HICK IS CHIC

◆

JEFF FOXWORTHY

◆

Illustrations by David Boyd

LONGSTREET PRESS

Atlanta, Georgia

Published by
LONGSTREET PRESS, INC.
2150 Newmarket Parkway
Suite 102
Marietta, Georgia 30067

Printed in the United States of America

1st printing, 1990

Library of Congress Catalog Number 90-061853

ISBN 0-929264-42-8

This book was printed by Ringier America, Olathe, Kansas. The text was set in Bookman Light by Typo-Repro Service, Inc., Atlanta, Georgia.
Cover illustration by David Boyd.
Book design by Jill Dible.

Dedication

To Elliott, for the idea, and
to Vic, for the direction

Acknowledgements

Thanks to my family for their never-ending support. And special thanks to a very special person, my wife, Pamela Gregg.

FOREWORD

"Mind your manners!"

I bet I heard that phrase a million times when I was growing up. Translated into Mom language, it always meant something like, "Quit trying to balance that fish stick on your nose!" or, "Get your underwear off your sister's head!"

For some reason these things always embarrassed my Mom. She wanted her friends, and even total strangers, to think that she had not failed in teaching us the correct way to conduct ourselves. But behaving in public was strictly for her benefit; we were just kids and immune to embarrassment.

Today, however, we all are a few years older, and now we realize that it's hard to make friends or climb the company ladder by making fools of ourselves in public places. Perhaps a friend has pointed out to you that the "Social Graces" are not members of a gospel singing group. It's no longer Mom you have to worry about embarrassing. It's yourself. Now we know we should have listened to her.

FOREWORD

Fortunately there is a solution to this problem . . . without having to admit that we were wrong. This little book, compiled through years of embarrassing research, contains enough basic tutoring in the social skills to allow you to attend the state fair without making a single *faux paw* [sic]. Guaranteed.

Mind your manners,

J.F.

P.S. No need to send me a thank-you note.

PERSONAL HYGIENE

BATHING — How Much, How Often

While lye soap is a quick-fix solution, it has been scientifically proven that regular bathing goes a long way towards a lice-free lifestyle.

I recommend bathing at home, instead of taking a bar of soap to the local YMCA. Cleaning the ring out of a swimming pool can take forever.

MANICURES AND PEDICURES

Sometimes you may find it impossible to chew a fingernail evenly. Don't panic. Household scissors or a sharp steak knife can usually handle the task. Toenails, however, present a tougher problem, and

PERSONAL HYGIENE

a strong wood file or boltcutters often provide the answer.
Remember to always put nail clippings in their proper place—the
ashtray.

PERSONAL HYGIENE

Dirt and grease under nails is a social no-no, as they tend to detract from a woman's jewelry and alter the tastes of finger foods.

Corns and Calluses

Foot surgery is a budget buster, but expensive doctor visits can often be avoided by doing certain procedures in the privacy of one's own home or automobile. For example, corns and calluses can be removed using a common potato peeler. Remember never to cut against the grain.

Polish

A coat of brightly colored polish can be very effective in drawing attention away from warts and open wounds, thus saving a girl unwanted embarrassment. It can also get a guy a great table in most restaurants.

PERSONAL HYGIENE

EARS

While ears need to be cleaned regularly, this is a job that should be done in private using one's *own* truck keys. (NOTE: Keys must also be cleaned regularly, because ear wax buildup can short-circuit a starter switch.) Post office keys are recommended for deep probing.

For serious wax buildup, do not rule out a garden hose as a hygiene partner.

HAIR CARE (Men)

Contrary to popular belief, dandruff is not an incurable disease. And despite what the guys around the gas pump say, shampooing regularly is not the leading cause of homosexuality (although apricot-scented shampoo *will* make you walk funny). Some women, in fact, actually find clean hair virile and attractive. For best results, brush hair before it dries completely.

PERSONAL HYGIENE

If you can afford store-bought hair tonic, use it. If, however, you're on a tight hygiene budget, many household items work just as well. Brake fluid, for example, not only holds the hair in place but also adds a dark, Elvis-like sheen to the scalp.

When talking sideburns, the word is big, Big, BIG!

PERSONAL HYGIENE

HAIR CARE (Women)

Sponge rollers (pink or green)
are a beauty tool no woman
should be without. They are not
without their disadvantages,
however. Rolling them too tight
can result in nasty headaches
and cause the eyes to dry out.
Also, a head full of rollers
dramatically reduces
a girl's chances
of talking her way
out of a traffic ticket.

PERSONAL HYGIENE

While a tall hive of hair is the current rage, it can be a high humidity hell as well as an open invitation to hornets and bees. A fifty-fifty mixture of Black Flag and hairspray can prove to be a girl's best summertime friend.

Your doo can be preserved by wrapping it in toilet paper. Save yourself unwanted embarrassment, however, by removing the tissue before leaving the house.

Hair color: Although blonde with black roots is the most popular color today, some trend-setters have gone to black with blonde roots. This effect can be achieved by squirting peroxide directly onto the scalp area with the use of a syringe. Red with black roots is also an acceptable option.

PERSONAL HYGIENE

EYEBROWS (Men)

When eyebrows reach the length where they obscure your vision, it's time to mow. Growing them long and combing them backwards to cover a receding hairline is not considered chic.

EYEBROWS (Women)

When plucking your eyebrows, start at the bridge of the nose and work earward. If not satisfied with the results, shave them off and draw on new ones using a waterproof marker — available in a variety of attractive colors.

NOSE HAIR

Plucking these unwanted devils
one at a time will work, but a
cigarette lighter and a small
tolerance for pain can
accomplish the same goal and
save hours. When using this
method, keep a bucket of water
nearby.

SHAVING (Men)

Electric razors are a modern inconvenience that I do not recommend. In the first place, electricity is not always available. And secondly, even if your razor is battery operated, swapping the batteries back and forth from your razor to your flashlight could leave you without a light on the roadside some dark night. You can't flag down help with a buzzing razor.

PERSONAL HYGIENE

The first rule of shaving is to take your time. A few days' contemplation is recommended. A man who is always clean shaven runs the risk of being labeled a sissy or a banker.

If you cut yourself while shaving, simply apply a small piece of toilet paper to the wound. If the bleeding has not stopped within twenty-four hours, a stitch or two may be required. (WARNING: Never apply a tourniquet to the neck.)

SHAVING (Women)

It is recommended that women occasionally shave their legs and underarms. No amount of effort, not even braiding, can make hair in these body regions attractive.

If shaving is required for the face as well, a woman should be very careful. A nasty scar can be just as unsightly as a moustache.

MAKE-UP

Good make-up, like a good paint job, requires a clean surface and a primer coat, and proper light is essential to obtaining this goal. You can't cover what you can't see. Fortunately, most bars are much darker than most bathrooms, and beer can be counted on to blur the vision of prospects. In most cases, an extra Bud can be just as effective as extra blush.

ORAL HYGIENE

BRUSHING

Scientists have proven that the use of a toothbrush (and toothpaste when available) can help people to keep their teeth into their thirties and even beyond. Many people brush on a daily basis. Each and every tooth should be brushed, no matter how far apart they are.

Unlike clothes and shoes, a toothbrush should never be a hand-me-down item.

ORAL HYGIENE

FLOSSING

Dental floss is the modern equivalent of broom straw. It can be purchased in most urban drugstores, but any loose thread on your clothing will work just as well and will tidy your appearance simultaneously. A lightweight monofilament fishing line also works wonderfully. I recommend removing all lures from the line before flossing.

COMMON SENSE ABOUT SCENTS

DEODORANT, PERFUME, COLOGNE, ETC.

Proper use of these toiletries can forestall bathing for several days. If the problem has escalated to the point that you are applying them directly to your clothing instead of to your skin, a bath is inevitable. If you live alone, deodorant is a waste of good money.

COMMON SENSE ABOUT SCENTS

MATCHES IN THE BATHROOM:
Covering Your Tracks

A host or hostess is expected to provide matches for the bathroom. I recommend spending the extra money for wooden matches; they are twice as effective as paper ones. A guest is not required to inform the group how many matches the performance demanded. *Any damages* resulting from explosion are the responsibility of the person who struck the match.

FASHION

GLOVES

A woman should always wear gloves with a full-length evening gown, as well as when she is handling rope or operating heavy machinery.

Do NOT wear rubber gloves in public, even if they do match your dress.

FASHION

JEWELRY

"It looks pretty but it turns my neck green!" This is a common complaint about 3K gold. If this is a problem for you, try other precious metals such as tin or aluminum. A little ingenuity can turn those beer can rings into a necklace you'll want to pass down to your grandchildren.

- Have your fine jewelry insured. If you lose one of the diamelles from your engagement ring, it can cost you . . . BIG! The premium on a $50 policy is less than the aggravation.

- Pearls with a tube top? Yes, they are an excellent example of understated elegance, but *never* before April.

FASHION

CLOTHING (Women)

In summertime, nothing accentuates a nice shoulder tattoo like a sundress. And here's how to make that listless butterfly really come alive: When you go to the river to sunbathe, cover the tattoo with some of your date's used chewing tobacco. The rest of your skin will turn a bright red when sunburned, but the tattoo will remain creamy white. The effect can be startling, making the butterfly appear to be in flight.

FASHION

- As for bathing suits, the expression "If you've got it, flaunt it!" does not apply to hips. A good rule of thumb is three square feet of fabric for every one hundred pounds. While flannel may feel good against your skin, avoid flannel bathing suits. They absorb a great deal of water and tend to sag even when you don't.

- No matter how durable, Army boots are not proper footwear for mothers. And hip waders are not considered dress pants.

FASHION

CLOTHING (Men)

This subject can be summarized in a single phrase:
No collar, no tie.

Care of Clothing

Sweat stains detract from the beauty of any dress, shirt, or suit. Since the salt deposits from such stains are not suitable for table use anyway, I recommend having your nice clothes professionally cleaned and pressed. An iron that's too hot can spell disaster for even the best double-knit.

DINING OUT

(NO SHIRT, NO SHOES, NO SERVICE . . .
THE HOITY RESTAURANTS)

There are times when women prefer eating a meal someplace other than on a TV tray or in a car. Since many dining establishments require shirts and shoes, such occasions may require advance planning by the man. I recommend keeping a clean pair of jeans and a fresh T-shirt in the trunk of your car. When properly positioned, these can also serve to keep the jack from rattling.

ORDERLY ORDERING

When dining out, it is not only acceptable for the man to order for his female companion, it is a recommended way of controlling the economic outflow for the evening. Nothing can be more embarrassing than having to counter your date's, "I think I'll have the deluxe platter," with, "Think again." When left to make her own decisions, a woman will always want a side order of French fries. As a matter of pure convenience, it is easier for the man to order since he is usually driving and is closer to the speaker.

GETTING THE WAITER'S ATTENTION

For unknown reasons, waiters are seldom waiting when you need one. Therefore, you must take measures to get their attention. If the waiter is only a couple of tables away, a sharp whistle will usually do the trick. If he is across the room, however, nothing solicits a quicker response than throwing a biscuit at his head. (NOTE: Throw only fresh biscuits. A man in Illinois connected with a day-old number and was charged with aggravated assault.)

DINING OUT

ORDERING WINE

In fancy restaurants, wine bottles usually come sealed with a cork instead of a screw-on cap. Consider this a bonus and pocket the cork for a future fishing trip.

DINING OUT

It is the responsibility of the person who orders the wine to taste it before serving it to others. The proper technique is to take a small sip and roll it around in your mouth. (NOTE: Gargling is frowned upon.) If the wine is bad, do not spit it out and yell, "Somebody forgot to wash their feet before they stomped these grapes!" Just swallow it and make a sincere effort to keep it down.

When decanting wine, make sure that you tilt the paper cup and pour slowly so as not to "bruise" the fruit of the vine. If drinking directly from the bottle, always hold it with your fingers covering the label.

TABLE CONVERSATION

Try to avoid any stories
about car wrecks,
operations, or sick pets.
Nothing ruins a good
meal quicker than
someone getting sick
or sentimental
at the table.

DINING OUT

While perfectly okay at home, it is considered crass when dining out to ask, "Are you gonna eat the rest of that meatloaf?" Especially if you don't know the person.

LEFTOVERS
("I paid for it. It's mine.")

At the end of a meal, it is perfectly okay to ask your waiter or waitress for a box ". . . so I can take these scraps home to my dog." Remember, however, to remove the small chicken bones and cold grits, as both can choke a dog in a heartbeat.

Many establishments frown on the use of a "doggie bag" at the all-you-can-eat salad bar. Avoid these pretentious places.

DINING OUT

TIPPING

Remember to leave a generous tip for good service. After all, their mobile home cost just as much as yours.

Commonly Asked Questions (and Answers):

Q: Where should you leave your silverware when you have finished eating?
A: Standing in your water glass.

Q: When is it proper to be seated?
A: After the hostess is seated, or whenever you feel gas coming on.

Q: What is the correct way to pass food around the table?
A: Overhanded, especially if you can put a nice spiral on a sweet potato.

DINING OUT

Q: Is it okay to dip your bread in gravy?
A: Only if it is on your own clothes.

DINING OUT

Q: Is it proper to reach across the table?

A: Yes, just as in shooting pool, as long as you keep one foot on the floor.

Q: What is too big a bite?

A: If you've got one end in your teeth and the other in your hand, and your hand is more than six inches from your mouth, that's too big a bite.

DINING IN OTHERS' HOMES

If your host or hostess has not
provided the proper instruments
for your culinary experience, it is
perfectly okay to remove your
personal knife or hatchet from
your belt and use it.

DINING IN OTHERS' HOMES

Many times you will need a good weapon for breaking large joints or hacking away at fur or fat. Often a choice morsel hides just beneath an inch or so of gristle. Do not, however, bang the handle of your knife with a ketchup bottle; you could damage the blade.

When you have finished using the knife, it should be wiped clean on the tablecloth and returned to its sheath or stuck into the table. Remember, however, that formica is very hard and can dull the tip of even the finest buck knife.

DINING IN OTHERS' HOMES

ADDITIONAL TIPS

- Wipe your feet before entering so you don't bring in what they sent the dog outside to do.

- When eating at a friend's home, it is generally considered rude to ask what a particular dish is. Besides, you may discover that you really don't want to know all the ingredients in "Roadkill Casserole."

- A loud burp at the table can be embarrassing for everyone. After such an incident, it is the host or hostess's responsibility to put the group at ease by saying something like, "Sounds better since you had it tuned."

DINING IN OTHERS' HOMES

Remember that not everyone thinks like you do. When visiting others, establish early in the evening what is okay and what is not okay to spit in.

OUT FOR THE EVENING

Sometimes you may find yourself in certain social settings where you don't know anyone. It can be extremely awkward trying to converse with strangers, so I have come up with a number of conversation starters. Here are a few lines proven effective in breaking the ice:

- How much do you want for that refrigerator on the front porch?

- My old lady wants to get to know you.

- Let's step out on the porch where the flies ain't so bad.

- Is that an extra-firm mattress on top of your car?

- I bought some pearls just like those at a yard sale last weekend.

- Whose feet stink?

OUT FOR THE EVENING

- Do I have anything stuck in my teeth?

- How long have you had that thing on your nose?

- Is that a new tattoo?

- When's your parole up?

ENTERTAINING IN YOUR HOME

As you climb the social and professional ladder, you will find yourself often entertaining guests. Following are tips to make sure their visit is a memorable one:

- Go the extra mile and take the trash out a couple of days before guests arrive. It is difficult to be witty when your nose burns.

- While a wise use of time, guests may feel snubbed if you continue to iron clothes while the group chats. Besides, the steam may cause a woman's make-up to run.

- Make your guests feel at home. Let them adjust the rabbit ears on the TV, and make the dog give up the couch.

ENTERTAINING IN YOUR HOME

- An alert host or hostess always provides an appetizer. A few cans of Vienna sausages, a Spam loaf, and a box of Ritz crackers can really start an evening off on the right foot. Be careful when serving leftovers. A good rule of thumb is, "If the dogs won't eat it, company probably won't either."

- Even if a guest is extremely talkative and dominating the conversation, refrain from saying, "How 'bout putting some teeth in that hole."

- If you have a clothesline in your front yard, it is in good taste to remove the clothes before receiving guests. Your underwear can tell others more than they really want to know about you.

- Always wipe your hands before picking your teeth.

A centerpiece for the table should never be anything prepared by a taxidermist.

ENTERTAINING IN YOUR HOME

During flood season, refrain from entertaining until all the water has receded from the living room.

ENTERTAINING IN YOUR HOME

- Do not allow your dog to eat at the table . . . no matter how good his manners are.

- A little imagination can make your home look its best. Cover those nasty burn holes in the carpet with strategically placed old newspapers or a basket of dirty clothes.

- Be considerate of your guests. Point out in advance where the injury-threatening springs are located on the sofa.

- If guests overstay their welcome, it may be necessary to give them hints that it's time to leave. I suggest a gentle reminder such as, "Y'all are either going to have to leave or chip in on the rent." If that doesn't work, call the law and report that you've got squatters.

ENTERTAINING IN YOUR HOME

Prepare your house for visitors. Nothing can bring conversation to a screeching halt quicker than the loud snap of a rat trap. If this social nightmare should occur, the host is not obliged to show the victim to the group . . . unless they ask to see it.

DATING (Outside the Family)

A good bloodline should be protected. Don't date or marry outside the family unless it's absolutely necessary. If all your cousins are taken and you're forced to look outside, here is some advice:

- Asking a woman for a date can be a nerve-wracking experience, because all men fear rejection. But just remember—if she doesn't say no to anyone else, she probably won't say no to you. A typical intro might be, "Hello, Sybil. This is Jimbo Crosswater. Your brother shot my brother, remember? Well, if you aren't busy Friday night, you want to go out to the farm and watch the cows mate?"

- Be aggressive. Let her know you're interested: "I've been wanting to go out with you since I read that stuff on the men's bathroom wall two years ago."

DATING (Outside the Family)

- Shower her with compliments: "You ain't near as ugly as your sister. And that scar barely shows when you get up close." Such praise will make her heart melt like margarine.

- One should always go to the door to pick up a date. An exception to this rule can be made if her family owns a dog that is currently involved in a civil suit, and the gentleman caller is unsure about how long or how strong the dog's chain is.

- Establish with your date's parents what time she is expected back. Some fathers might say, "Ten o'clock." Others might say, "Monday." If the answer is the latter, it is the boy's responsibility to get the girl to school on time.

- Double dating can be awkward if one of the couples is more promiscuous than the other. If the couple in the backseat happen to be the "rabbits," it is considered in poor taste to keep the

DATING *(Outside the Family)*

couple in the front seat informed of your progress. If the couple in the front seat cannot resist the dance of love, it is suggested that they at least stop the car.

- Be a gentleman: Always light your date's cigarette, cigar, or pipe.

- Spend your date dollars wisely. If a girl's name does not appear regularly on a bathroom wall, a water tower, or an overpass, odds are good that the date will end in frustration.

- Be considerate of your dating partner. Do not tell others the details of your intimate moments until after the date is concluded.

DATING (Outside the Family)

Even if you can't get a date, avoid kidnapping. It's bad for your reputation.

DATING (Outside the Family)

OTHER THINGS TO DO ON A DATE:

- Drink beer and watch TV
- Hang out around the liquor store
- Cruise the main drag

Sure, these are usually considered family activities, but they can also add a certain down-home quality to a date.

THEATER ETIQUETTE

- Crying babies should be taken to the lobby and picked up immediately after the movie has ended.

- Do not ask the concession stand attendant for the nacho cheese recipe.

- Do not eat popcorn or candy left over from the previous show.

THEATER ETIQUETTE

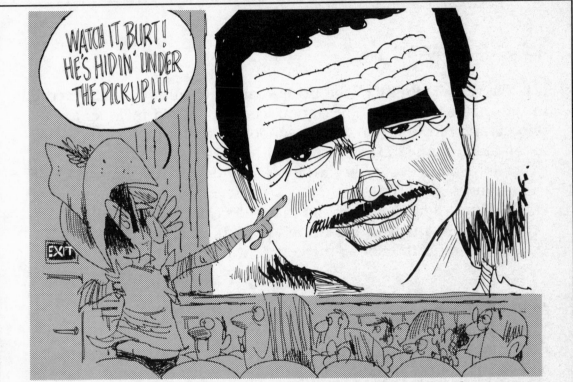

Refrain from talking to characters on the screen. Tests have proven that they can't hear you.

WEDDINGS

ANNOUNCEMENT

It is the responsibility of the bride's family to announce the wedding in the local newspaper. The announcement should include: a photograph of the bride (a high school yearbook picture is acceptable); name of the groom and his parents (if known); education completed by both the bride and groom (Do not include elementary school, unless that was the terminal degree); current employment (if applicable); and planned residence after the ceremony (If living with the bride's parents, it is not necessary to specify where in the house the couple will reside).

INVITATIONS

For planned weddings (at least nine months prior to a blessed event), any couple expecting to get a lot of free stuff must send out

WEDDINGS

invitations. They do not have to be lengthy. Something like, "You are invited to watch Scooter and Tracie make it legal on March 5th," will suffice nicely.

Invitations to short-notice weddings (less than nine months prior to a blessed event) may be delivered orally in a bar or on the work site by saying, "If you ain't doing nothin' Saturday, why don't you stop by for a cold one 'bout two o'clock. Me and Tracie's having some friends over to watch the ball game and witness our wedding."

PROPER ATTIRE

For the bride, the key phrase is, "Be conservative." No matter how good it may look, refrain from wedding outfits made with spandex or adorned with fringe. Excessive slits and dips also are frowned upon. This is not the day to show the world how big "they" are.

WEDDINGS

Here's another valuable hint: A bridal veil made of window screen is not only cost effective but also a proven fly deterrent.

For the groom, a rented tuxedo is haute couture, but if it means the difference between going on a honeymoon and staying home, consider some alternatives. For example, a leisure suit with a cummerbund and a clean bowling shirt can create a natty appearance. Though possibly uncomfortable, say yes to socks and shoes for this special occasion.

WEDDINGS

THE CEREMONY

No matter how urgent the event, loaded weapons have no place at the altar. And at the point in the ceremony that says, "If anybody has any reason why these two should not be joined in holy matrimony. . ." the preacher is advised not to pause too long. Old flames sometimes die hard and talk too much.

As the ceremony is concluded, the bride and groom are reminded that a short kiss will do. This is neither the time nor place to demonstrate their sexual expertise to the world. That's why they make VCRs.

WEDDINGS

RECEPTION TIPS

- Remember to reserve the VFW far in advance, and avoid Saturdays, since that's square dancing night.

- It is perfectly acceptable to ask guests to wipe their feet before entering the hall. After all, the cleaning deposit can be the difference between an oil change and a full tune-up for the pick-up.

- When going through the receiving line, it is proper to say something nice to the bride, such as, "Your baby is real cute."

- Stealing liquor from an open bar is a no-no.

- If someone asks where the bride is registered, do not answer, "The American Kennel Club."

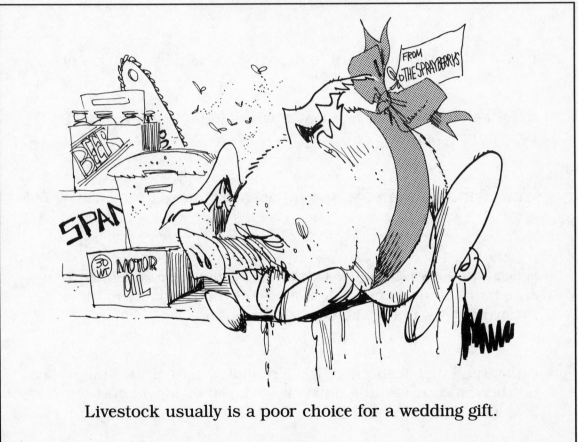

Livestock usually is a poor choice for a wedding gift.

WEDDINGS

- Kissing the bride for more than five seconds may get you cut.

- Never ask someone to be in your wedding if attending would violate their parole.

- When dancing, do not remove undergarments, no matter how hot it is.

- When throwing rice at the bride and groom, use uncooked rice and toss it underhanded. Never pocket the rice instead of throwing it, no matter how tough times are.

- If the wedding is cancelled, the girl should return the ring. If her brother has already killed the ex-groom, the ring should be returned to his next of kin.

WEDDINGS

OTHER COMMON WEDDING QUESTIONS

Q: Is it all right to bring a date to a wedding?
A: Not if you are the groom.

Q: How many showers is the bride supposed to have?
A: At least one within a week of the wedding.

Q: How many bridal attendants should the bride have?
A: One for each of her kids.

Q: What music is recommended for the wedding ceremony?
A: Anything except "Tied to the Whipping Post."

DRIVING ETIQUETTE

- Dim your headlights for approaching vehicles, even if the gun is loaded and the deer is in sight.

- Replace missing car doors as a courtesy to your passengers.

- When approaching a four-way stop, remember that the vehicle with the largest tires always has the right of way.

- Never tow another car using pantyhose and duct tape.

- Never play Chinese fire drill with handicapped passengers. Especially if parked on a hill.

- When sending your wife down the road with a gas can, it is impolite to ask her to bring back beer.

DRIVING ETIQUETTE

- Never relieve yourself from a moving vehicle, especially when driving.

- When traveling with a mattress on top of the car, do not allow others to take a nap on it.

- Never fish from a moving vehicle.

- Do not remove the seats from a car so that all of your kids can fit in.

- Never make catcalls at women in another car if a big guy is traveling with them.

When traveling
with your family,
try to keep their
"mooning" of other
drivers to
a minimum.

DRIVING ETIQUETTE

- Remember that the median is not a passing lane.

- Don't spit tobacco out of the window if you know the people following you.

- Do not lay rubber while traveling in a funeral procession.

- When towing a boat, insist that your fishing buddies ride inside the car.

- Never hit mailboxes with a baseball bat from a moving car. Especially in your own neighborhood. Someone might recognize you.

HOSPITAL ETIQUETTE

When receiving visitors in the hospital, the patient is not expected to show strangers his scars. Not everyone is fascinated by a vasectomy.

When visiting friends in the hospital, one should always bring his or her own beer. While it is perfectly acceptable to fill an infirmed friend's IV bag with a cold pop, one should never use a bedpan as a punchbowl.

FUNERALS

Never postpone a burial by placing your loved one in the freezer "until money's not quite so tight."

If you are asked to deliver a eulogy, remember that you're supposed to honor the deceased. That does *not* mean, however, that you brag about his sexual exploits, his ability to hold his liquor, or the time he wrote poetry on the side of the gymnasium with spray paint.

FUNERALS

It is considered improper to bury people on your own property . . . or anyone else's property without their permission. In either case, the authorities frown on it.

When viewing the body, never say, "He looks so natural. Like he just got drunk and passed out."

TIPS FOR ALL OCCASIONS

- Never allow a woman to walk through a mud puddle. Put her on your shoulders and carry her across.

- If a lady drops a handerchief, always pick it up for her. If it has been used recently, use a stick.

- Don't make company sleep on dirty sheets. Give them directions to the laundromat.

- Rugs need to be occasionally beaten, not just threatened.

- Never set off a flea bomb in someone else's home without asking first.

TIPS FOR ALL OCCASIONS

When giving birth, have a relative call your school so you won't be charged with an unexplained absence.

TIPS FOR ALL OCCASIONS

- Never go up to a stranger on the beach and ask if you can get that pimple on his back.

- Teach your children not to eat French fries found in other people's cars.

- It is considered tacky to take a cooler to church.

- No matter how broke you are, never take your date flowers that were stolen from a cemetery.

- If your dog falls in love with a guest's leg, have the decency to leave them alone for a few minutes.

- Always offer to bait your date's hook, especially on the first date.

- Even if you're certain that you are included in the will, it is considered tacky to drive a U-Haul to the funeral home.

TIPS FOR ALL OCCASIONS

Always identify people in your yard before shooting at them.

TIPS FOR ALL OCCASIONS

- Teach your children proper telephone etiquette. Nothing can be more embarrassing than hearing Junior say, "We ain't seen Daddy in eight days, and Mama's too drunk to come to the phone."

- Never ask someone else to hold your chew.

- Always say "Excuse me" after getting sick in someone else's car.

- Open and close doors quietly . . . if you have them.

- Don't put your feet on the table during dinner to show off your new half-soles.

- At a baby shower, never ask, "Do you have any idea who the father is?"

- When leaving town for the weekend, parents should not board their children at the local kennel.

TIPS FOR ALL OCCASIONS

Never take a beer
to a job interview.

TIPS FOR ALL OCCASIONS

- The socially refined never fish coins out of public toilets, especially if other people are present.

- Prank phone calls should cease after the age of thirty.

- If you have to vacuum the bed, it's time to change the sheets.

- When in public places, use public restrooms instead of the parking lot, potted plants, and balconies.

- One should tip a valet extra if he has to push or jump-start your car.

Always provide an alibi for family members.

Etiquette books are like condoms — everybody ought to have one even if they never use it.